Mindfulness
for children

How to raise your child to be grateful, serene, and self-confident with mindfulness training and awareness exercises - includes meditation.

Marieke Buschmann

CONTENT

What you can expect in this book

Mindfulness is currently on everyone's lips, and many people are undergoing a shift away from fast-paced life toward deceleration and awareness. Adults are beginning to meditate and to experience their everyday life more consciously and to be more mindful of themselves, their bodies and their fellow human beings. That's good. But mindfulness can also be a meaningful lifestyle for children and bring many positive effects for them.

In this book you will therefore first learn some general information about mindfulness, what it means, where it comes from and what inner attitude is helpful for it.

But the heart of the book is about your child, why mindfulness can be such a valuable tool even for children already, and what it can do to your child's self-image, self-awareness, self-confidence.

But in order to be able to practice mindfulness with your child in a meaningful and effective way, there are some framework conditions and prerequisites that can favor and promote the learning of mindfulness, the performance of mindfulness and concentration exercises, and the perception and conscious experience of your child. For this, you as a parent play an important role that should not be ignored. But also your attitude towards the child, the approach and trust are decisive for whether he or she can develop curiosity and openness for mindfulness and, if necessary, shed fears or prejudices.

In order to get started, the last chapter of this book contains numerous uncomplicated, practical examples suitable for everyday use and above all for children, mindfulness exercises and tips on how to carry them out, from physical exercises and sensory perception games to meditations suitable for children.

Mindfulness - explained in a nutshell

Mindfulness is currently a big buzzword and on everyone's lips. Social media, blogs and newspapers are full of mindfulness tips, from mindful breathing to conscious eating.

But mindfulness is not a new trend, but a meditation and attention practice that had its beginnings in early Buddhism. But more about that later.

First, it's important to know what mindfulness really means.

THIS IS WHAT MINDFULNESS MEANS?

"Mindfulness is consciously noticing in the here and now without judgment."

It is attentive listening to the world and to oneself, looking closely, discovering small things, consciously experiencing, recognizing, feeling, being. Mindfulness can be learned through practice in everyday activities and tasks, doing them consciously, without distraction or judgment. Every moment is an invitation to mindfulness.

Mindfulness also means seeing things, situations, people and oneself as they are, without necessarily wanting to change anything about them, but accepting them and making the best of them.

What mindfulness is based on, what inner attitude is behind it and how it can affect your child if practiced regularly, you will learn in the course of the next chapters.

THAT'S WHERE SHE'S FROM?

Mindfulness, as already mentioned, comes from Buddhism. While here it is predominantly associated with meditation as a method, in modern times mindfulness practice is no longer exclusively about meditation, but also about a range of attention and concentration exercises.

Other roots of mindfulness are in Eastern spiritual traditions, such as meditation, but also yoga and Zen.

This means that mindfulness can be practiced in very different ways. Meditation can be part of it, but does not have to be. There are many practical exercises in the practical part.

The 7 pillars of mindfulness

Jon Kabat-Zinn, a modern representative of mindfulness, has summarized the inner attitude on which it is based very clearly and easily understandable in "Seven Pillars of Mindfulness". They could also be described as the core values of mindfulness. These are non-judgment, patience, beginner's mind, trust, not-forcing, acceptance, and letting go. So to understand this better, it makes sense to take a closer look at these seven pillars:

NON-JUDGMENT

The first pillar of mindfulness is "non-judgment". In this case, not judging is equivalent to not evaluating, i.e. to perceive and observe value-free. We humans always tend to evaluate everything and everyone:n, including ourselves, our thoughts, feelings, etc. based on our experiences, patterns and beliefs. We are used to thinking in categories, and thus to judge some thoughts, feelings, people and situations as good, beautiful, wonderful or positive, and others as bad, terrible, unattractive and negative. In this way, our brain creates order in the flood of impressions that are constantly pelting us. If something or someone does not fit into these categories or cannot be clearly categorized, we become nervous.

At the same time, however, this also means that the attempt to stop judging altogether would fail anyway, because our brain is geared that way and even needs this judging and evaluating in order to cope. However, a mindful attitude and regular mindfulness practice can greatly help us to notice when we are judging. It is not necessarily a matter of not evaluating at all, but of noticing the evaluation and the thoughts about it and observing them first. If we notice that we have evaluated something, it is not a matter of judging this evaluation as bad, but simply to perceive it without reacting further to it or to move these evaluative thoughts on and, if necessary, to let them go.

So if we manage to perceive the evaluation, but let it move on afterwards, we allow ourselves to deal with situations and people in a less biased way, which we might otherwise have evaluated as negative, difficult or stressful. This opens up many more possibilities and ways for us to deal with these situations, people or even ourselves and everything that belongs to us. Challenges can turn into opportunities and "stress" into growth, because our view of things can change completely. On the subject of stress, there is an extra point in the course of the book.

PATIENCE

The second pillar of mindfulness is patience. Patience means (according to the dictionary) having "perseverance in calmly, controlledly, indulgently enduring or waiting for something." So it means that we accept and understand that everything takes its time and does not go faster the more we get angry or upset about it.

The blade of grass does not grow faster when you pull on it. In mindfulness, this means first and foremost that we may also be patient with ourselves. Yes, we may be as patient with ourselves as with the blade of grass, because mindfulness is a matter of practice and requires a lot of rest and time. Body and mind are allowed to slowly approach and get used to being more and more often completely in the moment, doing nothing and staying in the here and now without distractions, especially if body and mind are not used to that. Making this work is a process. A growth process like that of a blade of grass, and everyone grows at different rates.

This is roughly comparable to sports workouts, regular trips to the gym or running training. Here, too, the body must first slowly get used to the movement and the muscles only gradually become stronger and more defined and can be used more consciously and in a more targeted manner. Here we usually also do not expect that after only one work-out the belly becomes a six-pack or that we already have the endurance for a marathon after the first run. It is connected with training and needs just as much patience as mindfulness training.

So there will always be days when we find it difficult to focus (at first) and get distracted by external things or our own thoughts. This is okay and quite natural and therefore no reason to become impatient. The more often we practice mindfulness, the more often it will work and the more purposefully we can direct our minds. Being patient means giving ourselves time and not expecting too much of ourselves in the process.

The beginner's mind is the third pillar of mindfulness. It means looking at things, situations and people as if we were seeing them for the first time, completely free of our previous experiences, opinions and perspectives. These influence our truth and make us see everything we encounter through the glasses of our preconceived opinions.

But the beginner's mind allows us a change of perspective and a whole new, different way of looking at things. As a result, entrenched judgments can be dissolved or re-sorted.

We can free ourselves from expectations and ideas we had before and see completely new facets to which our eyes would remain closed if we did not use the beginner's mind. Similar to non-judgment, it's about looking at things in a different way again and broadening your horizons as a result.

There is a very simple exercise for this, which you can try very well alone, but also directly together with your child:

Take an everyday object from your household, such as a shoe, a glass, or one of your child's toys, and look at it as if you really had never seen it before. What do you notice about it under these circumstances? What color is the object? How does it feel? How heavy or light is it? What is the texture of the object? What does it look like? What does it smell like? Use all your senses to understand the object. But avoid judgmental descriptions like "the object stinks" or "it looks ugly. Observe yourself how you see the object now, after this detailed and objective observation. Has your view of it changed?

There are more mindfulness and attention exercises for your children (and yourself) later still in the practice section of the book.

TRUST

Trust is the fourth pillar of mindfulness. According to Duden's definition, trust is "the firm conviction of the reliability, dependability of a person or thing".

Mindfulness is primarily about trusting ourselves, our own abilities, feelings, thoughts and sensations. It's about gaining more confidence in ourselves, trusting our intuition, believing in our inner knowledge and listening to ourselves and our body. And to trust that our body sends us the right signals.

In the course of our lives, we are often deprived of this confidence and the abilities of our body. Every now and then, we are led to believe that other people know better than we do. Until at some point we prefer to rely on the statements and assessments of others who supposedly know better because they are experts in certain areas.

However, children in particular still have this trust in themselves, are unprejudiced and have not yet been exposed to so many evaluations. Therefore, it is incredibly important to continue to support them in trusting themselves. This is possible through mindfulness, more about this later.

It is also about trusting that we can be mindful at any time, that we will manage to live a mindful lifestyle, or for starters, experience our first mindful moments.

By the way, as we gain more and more confidence in ourselves, it will also affect our confidence in other people, in our relationships, and in the goodness of ourselves.

NOTHING-FORCING

The fifth pillar is "forcing nothing". In this context, this means not only not putting yourself under pressure and waiting impatiently for something to change, but also approaching the subject of mindfulness without expectations and goals, because mindfulness has no goals, such as becoming happier, more serene, more cheerful, more relaxed, or more profound. After all, these goals would always be linked to some intention and expectation. Expectations and intentions, however, are always connected with evaluations and thus are not the purpose of mindfulness.

But a regular mindfulness practice can very well bring positive effects if we stick to it. It is not a matter of forcing these positive effects or actively working towards them, but rather of being "oneself" without any intention or goal, because then these positive effects will arise over time without any coercion, intention or pressure. Which positive effects this can be (especially for children), I will go into more detail later.

ACCEPTANCE

Acceptance, that is, accepting people, situations and oneself, is the sixth pillar of mindfulness.

This is not about resignation, but really about acceptance and acceptance. There are many things in life, such as illness, separation, death, which we cannot influence. However, we often fight against them and waste a lot of valuable time and equally valuable energy. However, it is also part of the natural process to struggle and deny what cannot be changed. But little by little we can learn to come to terms with reality. And that is acceptance. Acceptance means relaxing into what is and accepting ourselves and the present moment as it is.

The German Lutheran theologian Friedrich Oetinger formulated an apt saying in this regard, which is very well known today and is often quoted:

"Give me serenity to accept things I cannot change; give me courage to change things I am capable of changing, and give me wisdom to distinguish one from the other."

So acceptance also means coming to terms with what is and making the best of it.

LET GO

Letting go is an important basic requirement of mindfulness. We tend to want to hold on to positive experiences, feelings, sensations and thoughts, conserve them forever and never let them go, because we realize that they are good for us.

It's different with unpleasant experiences and feelings. We would like to get rid of them immediately, never think about them again and banish them from our memory. We would also like to avoid them in the future.

That is, some things we cling to and do not want to release, and others we in turn reject and cannot accept.

Sometimes, however, we forget that the nice thoughts and feelings are not responsible for our well-being and happiness, but that this comes out of ourselves and that we do not need them for this at all. And that, conversely, the unpleasant thoughts and feelings are not to blame for our discomfort or unhappiness.

So letting go is about perceiving both the beautiful and the unpleasant thoughts and feelings in a non-judgmental way, observing them and letting them move on. By doing this, we accept that everything is transient and nothing lasts forever. And we become aware that our thoughts and feelings are not the same as our happiness or unhappiness, joy or suffering, well-being or discomfort.

Why mindfulness is so important in children's every-day lives

As mentioned earlier, mindfulness has no goals in that sense, but it can lead to helpful and positive effects in terms of personal development, self-image, confidence in oneself, and how one looks at things if practiced regularly.

Even children are already exposed to many stimuli, tasks and demands. Their world is now almost as fast-paced as that of adults. In daycare and school, they have to find their way into a system, and an unbelievable number of impressions, experiences and adventures pelt them every day.

And they grow up in a world in which media are omnipresent. This has wonderful advantages, but also brings one or two challenges with it, because the use of media such as TVs, tablets, etc. provides them with yet another multitude of stimuli that need to be processed.

All of this can certainly lead to stress, excessive demands or exhaustion. So it makes sense to teach children at an early age to be mindful of themselves, their own resources and needs, their own bodies and feelings.

DEALING WITH STRESS IN A HEALTHY WAY

As mentioned earlier, our children, just like us adults, live in a rapidly changing and accelerating world. And because of the demands, for example at school, our children could theoretically always be busy. With homework, learning, but also hobbies, appointments, etc.

To a certain extent, this kind of busyness is fine, but it's a tightrope walk between pleasant and manageable living and leisure and overwork.

What your child (and every other person) perceives as stressful is very subjective here, because first of all there are no stressful situations per se. It is only our evaluations of situations that make them stressful. And we form our evaluations, as already mentioned at the beginning of the book, through our experiences, imprints and patterns.

So if a kindergarten child has had a bad experience at gymnastics once in the daycare center, for example because he or she couldn't run as fast as the others or because he or she was scolded for not changing quickly enough, this can become an imprint. And the child can evaluate this situation "gymnastics" in the future as a stressful situation or as an unpleasant situation if this situation was very striking for him.

Children also have a variety of experiences at school that lead to "negative" evaluations and cause stress when repeated.

I.e., your child's evaluation accordingly influences his or her response to these individual experiences and situations.

Through a mindful view, which is at best not judgmental but observing of these situations, the stress reaction can be influenced, weakened or the judgment of it can even be dissolved.

By practicing mindfulness regularly, your child learns to pause and observe his or her own thoughts and feelings about individual situations in a non-judgmental way. This means that it is more and more able to take advantage of the brief moment between the occurrence of the supposed stressful situation and the stress reaction and to break this cycle of evaluation and patterns.

S CHULNG OF CONCENTRATION AND ATTENTION

Children need to be very focused and attentive even at daycare. There are already many activities that require this of them. But the whole day-to-day life in a group also requires that. At school, of course, this goes even further and becomes more specific.

Training concentration and attention at an early age therefore makes a lot of sense. Mindfulness exercises are in themselves nothing more than a series of concentration and attention exercises. The effect of these exercises is that your child is able to focus on one thing at that moment, such as his or her breath, senses, etc., and that even if he or she is momentarily distracted, he or she can come back to that attention. The more often your child practices this in mindfulness exercises, the easier it will be for him or her to call on this ability in everyday situations or at daycare/school.

VALUE-FREE PERCEPTION OF FEELINGS AND THOUGHTS

Dealing with one's own feelings can be challenging at times. Especially at a young age, children first have to gain emotional competence.

Here, regular mindfulness practice can help children learn to recognize, feel, and name their feelings. These three skills are still very complex for (young) children. If they then also have or have had bad experiences with acting out their feelings and have internalized initial, less helpful beliefs, children find it even more difficult to also accept their feelings in a non-judgmental way, because they have already been evaluated in other ways beforehand. Here are a few examples for the evaluation of children's feelings: "An Indian knows no pain" or "Boys don't cry" or "Everything is not so bad", although the situation felt very bad for the child.

But, as described above in dealing with stress, regular mindfulness training can help your child recognize and resolve these prior experiences and evaluations that have shaped your child through him or herself or from outside sources.

In addition, it is important for your child that you as a parent also accompany and mirror your child's feelings as non-judgmentally as possible. This helps your child to become even more aware of his or her feelings through mirroring and naming them on your part.

SELF-AWARENESS AND SELF-CONNECTEDNESS

Which brings us to the next point, self-awareness and self-connectedness. As should be clear by now, mindfulness is about conscious perception. That is, consciously noticing things around us, such as sounds, smells, people, moods, and so on. But it is also about perceiving ourselves, our own body, our own thoughts, feelings, moods, needs, worries and pain.

That is, to be aware of oneself, with everything that belongs to us. This often sounds so self-evident, but in our fast-moving times, the distractions and leisure opportunities are so varied that many people are increasingly preoc-cupied with the outside and less and less with themselves, that is, their inner selves. Your child is also growing up in this time and is exposed to it. This definitely has many advantages and opens up numerous possibilities for your child in terms of leisure activities, ways of learning, etc.

Nevertheless, it does no harm if your child learns at an early age to deal with himself as well, because a good self-confidence has a positive effect on his own self-image, self-confidence and, indeed, self-awareness.

It can be equally helpful for your child's development if he has a good connection to himself and his body. A good body awareness and also self-compassion are the result. Both are helpful qualities in a child's daily life. And a regular mindfulness practice with mindfulness exercises towards bodywork and conscious awareness of one's own body and mind support this greatly.

Getting started with mindfulness with children - how?

So before you start practicing mindfulness together with your child, it is important to learn something about the prerequisites and framework for mindfulness practice in general and mindfulness, concentration and attention exercises in particular. There are, in fact, some sensible things to consider in order to facilitate the child's entry into and first contacts with mindfulness.

NO RIGHT OR WRONG

First of all, it is really important for me to emphasize emphatically that there is no right or wrong in mindfulness. And you should also convey this feeling to your child at all times. Your child doesn't need to be afraid of failing or being "bad" at it. Since mindfulness wants to be without judgments, so there should be no judgments such as "You didn't meditate long enough," "You didn't exhale deeply enough," or "You're not sitting still, stop fidgeting." To categorize something as right or wrong would therefore be a judgment that does not belong here and would not be helpful.

Your child should come into contact with itself in a playful way, become aware of itself and be allowed to practice being completely itself. Joy, trying things out, doing things, observing and perceiving are the most important things here. However, this is only possible in a non-judgmental, safe environment that gives your child freedom and space to experiment.

And you yourself should not put pressure on your child or yourself in any way. Every person approaches the topic of mindfulness somewhat differently and takes different lengths of time to find his/her path and exercises that suit him/her particularly well. And, as mentioned earlier, mindfulness has no goals. So you can safely let go of high expectations of yourself, your child, or mindfulness itself, if any.

Your task as a parent is solely to accompany, to be available for your child's questions, to be open and curious, and to be yourself.

When this freedom from values is made clear to the child, he can learn to develop and live out himself and his mindfulness without pressure and coercion and with joy and curiosity.

ATMOSPHERE OF TRUST AND VOLUNTARINESS

Children who are allowed to try something new or are confronted with new things can react to it in two different ways. Some are very curious, open and approach things uninhibitedly right from the start. They can hardly wait to get started and have little shyness or fear of contact from the ground up.

However, there are also children who are rather cautious about new activities or experiments, especially if they do not yet know exactly what to expect. As described in point 4.1, they quickly worry about doing something wrong or simply don't have the confidence to do it at first.

Especially these children then need an atmosphere of trust. Someone like you as a parent who supports them, takes them by the hand and creates a non-judgmental space in which they don't have to have any worries, fears or concerns. Mindfulness or mindfulness exercises can sometimes be something very intimate, because children are allowed to learn to feel themselves, to be themselves. But they only dare to do this if there is no pressure, no evaluation or even judgment from the outside. They must feel safe and understood and accepted as they are, because only then can they develop their own being and discover it without fear.

That's why voluntariness also plays a crucial role here. Be in dialogue with your child, ask him what he feels like doing, which mindfulness exercises he likes and when he would like to try them. Mindfulness should be voluntary, from the inside out. Of course, it makes sense to stimulate and arouse the children's curiosity, to present and explain mindfulness and the associated exercises and values clearly. But this should be done in such a way that they do not feel persuaded or even pressured to try it out. Mindfulness training should be based on voluntariness and primarily come from the child. Only in this way can the child fully engage with it, let go and experience the moment consciously and without distraction.

PRINCIPLE OF SELF-DETERMINA-TION

As mentioned in the previous point, the child should be allowed to decide for itself at any time which mindfulness offers and exercises it would like to take advantage of and try out, and what it is confident enough to do. It would not be pedagogically valuable if the child were persuaded to participate.

The decision should therefore always lie with the child. As a parent, however, you always have the opportunity to make it easier for your child to try out and decide to practice mindfulness by selecting or, better yet, suggesting exercises that you are relatively sure would appeal to your child and would not be too much of a challenge for him or her. You know your child, his interests and preferences best and can respond or react sensitively accordingly.

If children are not pushed or put under pressure, they usually know very well what they want and can express this well and understandably at a relatively early age. They know themselves what is best for them at that moment and instinctively make the right decision. Being able to do this, by the way, is also already very mindful, and your child should therefore definitely be encouraged to do so and supported by you in this respect.

Especially anxious and cautious children should be accompanied very sensitively and allowed to start gradually and with small, very manageable exercises. The child sets the pace. If he or she then realizes after a mindfulness exercise that nothing bad can happen and that he or she can do nothing wrong, as described above, your child will take courage and gradually become more open and willing to experiment.

TOGETHER MINDFUL

For your child, it can be an unfamiliar and somewhat uncomfortable situation if he or she is practicing mindfulness and you are sitting next to him or her as a "spectator. He or she may feel observed and thus be inhibited from being himself or herself and experiencing the moment consciously and mindfully.

So there are two ways to deal with this: You offer your child a mindfulness exercise, explain the process, and then let them try it on their own. Some children actually prefer this and like to have their quiet time while doing it, so they can listen to themselves better and go at their own pace. Alternatively, just do the mindfulness exercises and practice mindfulness together with your child. This can have many benefits for your child, as well as for you:

For one thing, your child will not feel left alone with it and joint activities (no matter what kind) always create connection and closeness between you and your child.

In addition, you can exchange with each other during or after the exercises, report to each other what you felt and how you experienced the exercise. However, this should remain voluntary, because not every child or even you yourself necessarily want to disclose all feelings, sensations and thoughts. That is okay and also part of the protected space and the atmosphere of trust. Everyone decides for themselves what they want to share and what they want to keep to themselves.

By doing the exercises together with your child, you can also avoid giving your child the feeling that he or she is being judged or observed, or that you are already "better" at it than he or she is and don't need to practice at all. He or she might otherwise feel "belittled". When doing things together, you both have the same starting position and even if you lead or guide through one or the other exercise, a sense of community and equality is created that can help your child.

And if your child is particularly cautious or anxious, your participation can also help them shed any fears or insecurities.

And of course, practicing mindfulness can be helpful for you as well, because not only children but also adults can benefit from the positive effects described in the previous chapter.

REGULARITY IS THE KEY

One point is still missing before you can start practicing mindfulness with your child. It is important to point out that mindfulness can be particularly helpful and can quickly have positive effects if it is practiced and trained regularly. I have already compared the pillars of mindfulness with a sports workout, and that fits well here, too. No marathon runner has trained sporadically only once or a few times before. He/she is only so fit to run 42 km because he/she trains regularly for it.

It is similar with mindfulness training. Regularity creates commitment and a certain routine that can be helpful and motivating. But I will discuss the topic of routines and rituals in the next chapter.

So to establish a regular mindfulness routine, it makes sense to do a mindfulness exercise with your child once a day. This doesn't have to be long; 2-5 minutes is perfectly sufficient for the beginning. Gradually, at the child's pace, the duration can be increased if necessary.

Now the question may arise whether this regularity does not create pressure and whether voluntariness and self-determination suffer as a result.

It depends a lot on how you handle it as a parent. Of course, a regular mindfulness routine makes sense for reasons already mentioned. However, the playful aspect should not be lost for your child and there should still be no compulsion. So if your child doesn't feel like it in the meantime, you don't have to persuade him or her to join in.

Just do a mindfulness exercise yourself. Ideally, one that your child usually quite likes. And invite your child to join you beforehand if he or she decides to do it after all. The fact that you do the exercise anyway and thus maintain the regularity has several positive effects:

First, keep at it yourself and practice mindfulness regularly. This does no harm and will help you in your own mindfulness practice.

In addition, you act as a role model for your child and show, without pressure, that mindfulness is a natural part of your everyday life.

Children learn by example and also see what mindfulness does to you.

And even if your child doesn't want to join in that day, he or she may have the desire to join in again in a few hours or the next day.

Practical implementation possibilities in everyday life and practical examples and exercises

Now you can really start practicing mindfulness for your child and, if applicable, for yourself as well. In the following, I describe several ways in which mindfulness can be integrated into the everyday life of your child and the whole family in a practical and uncomplicated way. There are helpful examples in which form and in which everyday situations small mindfulness exercises make sense, and in each case you will find some easy-to-implement and child-friendly mindfulness exercises and practical examples. Have fun browsing and trying them out.

RITUALS AND ROUTINES

As already mentioned in the previous chapter, regular mindfulness practice is particularly effective and helpful. Rituals and routines can help to internalize and deepen mindfulness and the inner attitude toward it.

Rituals are very helpful for children. They provide orientation and security. Through them, the day gets a sequence and structure, just as it can be with the practice of mindfulness.

By establishing recurring mindfulness rituals, they will become routines after a while. Your child no longer has to think about whether and when to do which mindfulness exercises. It is already so internalized that it is part of the daily routine like brushing teeth or getting dressed and undressed.

It is not for nothing that the definition of routine (according to Duden) is as follows: "A routine is an ability, acquired through prolonged experience, to perform a particular activity very safely, quickly, and superiorly."

Observe which mindfulness exercises your child particularly likes and at which times of the day he or she is especially ready or receptive for them. Of course, depending on their age, you can also involve your child here and develop rituals together.

So it could be that you introduce a ritual in the morning that wakes your child up, gets the body going and lets your child arrive in the here and now already in the morning, or you always do the same mindfulness exercise (or a few varying exercises) after daycare or school or even in the evening to be able to switch off well and end the day.

The more often and regularly you do these exercises as a ritual, the faster it will become a routine and you will see that very soon your child will demand these rituals himself.

You will get some ideas about which exercises these could be in the further course of this chapter.

ENABLING AND SHAPING TRANSITIONS

A day in the life of a child consists of many small and larger transitions. It starts with waking up. This is a transition from sleep to wakefulness. It continues with getting out of bed and getting dressed. This is followed by the transition from the breakfast table to the bathroom and then from home to school or kindergarten. This continues throughout the day.

Transitions can present children with challenges. After all, each time they have to break away from one situation and move on to a new one. What sounds natural to us is a major achievement for our children. But even adults find it difficult time and again to make the transition from work to home, for example, without still being mentally at work or thinking about the next to-dos for the next day.

If these transitions are not consciously perceived, the children may firstly find it even more difficult and secondly quickly become overstimulated and overwhelmed by them.

But there are mindful ways to make or shape these transitions consciously.

Support your child in this process by allowing him or her to consciously notice these transitions and thus better move from one moment to the other.

This can be done very well by repeatedly drawing your child's attention to the fact that a situation is just ending and a new one is beginning. Pause for a moment with your child and briefly reflect together. This allows your child to say goodbye to the previous situation. Afterwards, it is often easier for him or her to move on to the next one.

It also slows down and helps your child and yourself to hurry through the day less quickly, because this brief pause already feels like a break. And even if it's short, your child's body and mind still have a little breather.

CONSCIOUS USE OF THE FIVE SENSES

The human being has five senses. These are hearing (auditory), sight (visual), touch (haptic), smell (olfactory) and taste (gustatory). We perceive our environment with these senses. With them we comprehend and grasp it and ourselves.

Mindfulness is about perceiving and observing, so the senses also play a very big role here. They help us to find our way in the world, and they can also provide or support wonderful moments and mindful moments.

As soon as we use our senses consciously, we are already mindful. Children love sensory exercises, which can therefore also be great mindfulness exercises. There are numerous and varied ways to practice mindfulness with children. A small selection of exercises follows now:

Eavesdropping concert

As the name suggests, this exercise is about listening. You can do it with your child both indoors and outdoors.

Sit down comfortably with your child. Outside, this can be on a bench or meadow, or inside on the couch or floor. Now set an alarm clock so that it rings after one minute.

If desired, the eyes can be closed. This often helps to concentrate better on hearing. Not all children like this or can do this, so your child may decide for himself how he wants to handle this.

Now listen attentively with your child to the surrounding sounds for one minute.

When the alarm clock rings, you and your child open your eyes and tell each other what you heard.

It's often amazing how many sounds there are to hear when you concentrate on them. Normally, our brain automatically filters out "unimportant" sounds so that we no longer notice them. Only when we consciously listen do we notice them.

It is also interesting to note how different the sounds can be depending on where and when you do this exercise.

The point here is only to perceive the sounds and describe them in a value-free way.

I see what you do not see
This game is very well known. Nevertheless, I explain it briefly:

One of the players says: "I see something that you don't see and that is ... [insert color]". At the same time, he picks out an object in the room in his mind that has this color.

The other players must now guess which object is meant.

In this case, you can alternate with your child who has to guess.

This game is about looking closely, consciously looking to see what objects are present in the color. Often it is the same here as with sounds: The brain filters out what is supposedly "unimportant" and we only see it when we concentrate on it.

This mindfulness game can also be done anywhere and be a great sensory game and pastime at the same time, even on the go.

Touch game

The touch game is obviously about feeling, that is, the sense of touch. For this, you as a parent can fill a box or shoebox with 3-5 objects (depending on the age of the child). Make sure they are made of different materials and have different textures. Examples: Stone, small cuddly toy, marble, puzzle piece, chestnut, pencil, brush, ball of wool, building block or similar.

Now spread a cloth over the box and place it on the table or on the floor.

Your child may now reach under the cloth into the box and feel an object from it without taking the cloth away or taking the object out of the box. If he or she wishes, he or she can try to describe the object, whether it is soft or hard, smooth or rough, large or small, round or square, etc. The point here is not to guess immediately what the object is, that is not important. The mere perception, feeling and describing are absolutely in the foreground here.

Therefore, even after extensive touching, the object remains in the box and is not looked at or uncovered.

Now the child can touch and feel the objects one after the other in this way, or you can take turns with your child. Then you feel the next object and describe to your child what you feel.

This has the advantage that your child learns from you to find descriptions and terms for what he or she feels. Often children still have a limited vocabulary, depending on how old they are.

Afterwards, feel free to talk to your child about how it was for you to feel the objects without being able to see them. Your child may also want to tell you how it felt.

Trick or treat

This is a taste game. For this, prepare a plate with different foods. Ideally, one of them should be sweet, one sour and one salty. Sweet foods could be sweets such as gummy bears, chocolate, cookies or similar. For the sour flavor, citrus fruits such as lemon or lime are suitable, and for the salty part, you can provide salty pretzels, for example.

Ask your child which food he or she would like to try first. Do not discuss the taste in advance. Incidentally, it is not a problem if your child already knows the foods and which tastes like which. In the spirit of the "beginner's mind" (see 2.3.), this exercise can be done without bias or judgment.

Once your child has decided on one of the foods, try them both. It is important that you and your child taste it consciously and really perceive the taste. To do this, it is advisable not to eat the food too quickly, but to move it back and forth in your mouth and chew for a long time. This is the best way for the taste to develop.

You can then talk about the taste experience. Try to talk about it as non-judgmentally as possible and rather describe it.

This exercise can be repeated with the foods of the other flavors. If you or your child don't want to try one of the foods at all, that's okay too. Perhaps you will then also find an alternative.

Smell memory

This game requires a little more preparation if you do not want to buy a ready-made olfactory memory in stores. You can use several bags for this. Always fill two bags with the same objects, herbs or scents. For example, lavender flowers, mint leaves, paper leaves dusted with perfume, coffee beans or similar are suitable for this.

Now close the bags with a ribbon and mark the matching bags inconspicuously with a small sign. Or do not close the bags so tightly so that you can easily open them later for checking.

Of course, you can also make the smelling memory together with your child.

Then you can put out all the bags and together with your child sniff out which bags belong together. As with the other sensory exercises, the primary goal is not to find out what the individual bags smell like, but to find out which ones belong together and how they smell.

Sensory walk

The previous examples have always focused on a single sense. In the sensory walk, all senses are used equally or one after the other.

Take your child for a walk in nature. Maybe you have a park, lake or forest nearby where you can try it out.

During the walk itself, go through one sense at a time with your child. For example, start with the sense of sight. Tell each other what you can see, for example, a squirrel, a snail, a beautiful flower, a mushroom.

Let's continue with hearing. What do you and your child hear? For example, birds chirping, wind rustling, leaves rustling, a woodpecker, dogs barking.

You can also smell a lot on a walk. So concentrate completely on your sense of smell for a while, too. What do you smell, what does your child smell? Maybe it smells like fresh grass, rain, animals or earth.

Next, take up the sense of touch with your child. How does the trunk of the tree feel or the ground under your feet? Depending on the weather, it can also be helpful to walk barefoot.

Last but not least, the sense of taste may also be put to use. Maybe you or your child will find a wild berry or taste a raindrop falling from the sky.

Thus, your child and yourself have made a walk for the senses.

Part of the practice of mindfulness is to perceive and accept oneself and one's own body in a mindful and non-judgmental way. The more mindfully we can feel into it, the better we understand its signals. In this way, children can better recognize when they should rest or how much strength they still have. But the improved body awareness also triggers a certain sense of well-being and creates trust in oneself and one's own body.

That is why there are numerous physical exercises that you can do together with your child.

Body parts knock awake
This exercise is well suited for your child's morning routine, as it invigorates the body and mind, in addition to allowing your child to arrive within themselves and their body.

Stand with your child hip-width apart and begin to gently tap all parts of the body with your hands, one after the other. Start with the head. Continue with the face, neck, chest, arms, stomach, back, buttocks, thighs, calves and feet.

Everyone decides for themselves how gentle or intensive the tapping should be. Of course, the head and face should be tapped more gently. With the legs or arms, for example, it can also be a little stronger. You can also play and experiment with the strength and intensity.

Quietly linger for a minute per body part so that you and your child can really go into awareness. If you move on too quickly, the body experience may have been too fleeting. Also make sure that you both consciously tap one body part after the other and concentrate fully on it, so that you really stay in the moment and do not already think about the next body part.

This exercise, i.e. tapping from head to toe, can then also be repeated once or twice.

Tapping activates the individual parts of the body and stimulates blood circulation. Therefore, the body may feel different afterwards than before. Feel free to talk with your child about how it feels, how the body feels afterwards. Describe your perception of this to each other.

Shake out body parts
This exercise, on the other hand, is more suitable for the evening, e.g. before going to bed. It should help to process the events of the day and to be able to conclude or let go, and promotes relaxation.

Here, stand again hip-width apart opposite each other. Now begin to shake out all parts of the body one after the other. Again, you and your child start at the head and work your way down to the tips of your toes. To be able to shake out the legs better, you and your child can also sit or lie down on the floor and shake out the legs and feet in the air.

Here your child can also imagine what it wants to shake off from this day, what it wants to let go of and shake out. In this way, with the help of the body exercise, he or she can bring the day to a good close and process what he or she may have found exhausting, stressful or annoying, and you can do the same, of course. If your child wants, he or she can also say out loud what he or she wants to shake off. You should leave the intensity of the shaking up to your child; after all, some experiences may need to be shaken up a little more vigorously and others a little less.

After shaking, the body may feel different again, similar to tapping. Perhaps warmer. Talk to your child about how the body feels and what the exercise has done to his mind as well. Of course, only when your child is ready for it.

GRATITUDE PRACTICE

Gratitude is an important tool for mindfulness, because through it we come back to the here and now from possible everyday worries or musings about the past. Because gratitude is a feeling that is present. Even children can have everyday worries and worries about the future, such as school issues, arguments with friends, or thinking about the past that they can't really change.

A gratitude routine can bring the focus back to what is and away from what was or will be.

And it reminds us of what is going well. Even with children, some days the good experiences and joyful events can quickly be pushed aside or buried by stressful situations or less pleasant things. So at the end of the day, they may judge the day as "bad" or "not nice" because the negative feelings and thoughts predominate or are more prevalent as a result. This is exactly why it is so important to recall the beautiful experiences again, so that they do not get lost in the possible stress of everyday life and the day is then remembered as "more beautiful" than initially assumed.

For adults, there is a large selection of gratitude diaries and journals available for purchase in stores for these purposes, and there are now also more and more offerings for children. But there is no need for ready-made gratitude books, and certainly not for children. In the following, I present two simple but beautiful ways to practice gratitude with children.

Gratitude coloring block

Gratitude can already be practiced and addressed regularly with very young children from about 3 years of age. However, children between the ages of 3 and 6 cannot usually write yet, so a gratitude diary naturally does not yet make sense for this age group.

If your child is kindergarten age, you could get a coloring pad with blank pages instead of a journal. Your child will be especially happy if he or she is allowed to choose one. If necessary, you can also design a gratitude block yourself.

As a ritual, you could then talk about the day together with your child in the evening, e.g. before going to bed. To end the day well and, above all, with a positive feeling, you should focus on the day's pleasant experiences.

This does not mean, by the way, that negative or stressful events should simply be hushed up or repressed - quite the opposite. Of course, your child should also be able to express these, discuss them with you and thus come to terms with them. But perhaps there is a more suitable time for this than shortly before falling asleep, because this can quickly lead to a thought carousel again.

So in the evening, ask your child what he or she is especially grateful for today. Your child can then draw the answer to this question in his or her gratitude coloring book.

Of course, you can also participate yourself by either also having your own gratitude coloring pad to draw in at the same time, or by writing your own response in a notebook.

Afterwards, you could tell each other about your gratitude. In this way, you and your child can also enter into an exchange that creates a connection. By retelling and describing the beautiful moments, they take on more weight and you can share in the joy with your child. This should again be done voluntarily, because children do not want to share every experience with their parents.

Depending on your child's age and concentration span, you can optionally ask another question:

What are you proud of today?

Or alternate the questions or simply let your child decide in the evening before the exercise which question they want to answer or draw on today.

If your child is already of school age and can already write, he or she can of course also keep a gratitude diary. But even here, some children still have a lot of joy in drawing.

Gratitude treasure chest

For adults, there is the ritual of the happiness jar. They collect all their moments of happiness in a jam jar by writing them on a slip of paper and placing them in the jar. This way they can't be forgotten and you can always remember them again by taking the little happiness notes out of the jar every now and then and reading through them again.

You can also do this exercise in a very similar form with your child. For children, the word happiness is often still a bit too abstract. Even many adults still have problems grasping this and defining happiness as such. But children are often more familiar with gratitude. They know what "thank you" means and when to say it. And so they can also understand that they can be grateful for beautiful moments, experiences or encounters.

Collecting these moments of gratitude is nice because the children can fish them out of their jar again at any time and reread them. Again, the younger children can also draw on what they are grateful for if they can't write yet.

And instead of a jar, it is recommended to use a nice box, crate or box for younger children. So it should be a sturdy container that can not break. This can of course be beautifully designed in advance by you or your child. Because the gratitude moments can also be seen like little treasures, the box can also be called a "gratitude treasure chest".

Similar to the gratitude coloring book, you can now talk to your child in the evening about what he or she is grateful for and place these moments in the form of slips of paper in his or her gratitude box. Again, you can join in and create your own gratitude box.

If your child is not yet familiar with the concept of gratitude, the question can also be:

What were you particularly happy about today?

MEDITATION

Meditation is a form of mindfulness practice, if not THE mindfulness practice par excellence. It is often associated or confused with esotericism. However, meditation is simply an exercise of attention and concentration that can train the inner peace, calm the mind and bring deceleration.

Children are also exposed to many impressions and distractions that come with our fast-paced times. Through meditation, your child can be itself, arrive in the here and now. He or she can leave all worries behind for a moment and stop or slow down possible thought carousels.

This is not about not having thoughts. Your child is not doing anything wrong if thoughts keep coming up. Rather, it's about noticing these thoughts and letting them move on and bringing

the focus back to yourself, e.g., through breathing or the senses.

If you would like to try meditating with your child, or if your child would like to, then he or she probably doesn't need that much explana-tion. Children are still very intuitive by nature. Talk to your child afterwards about how they felt about the meditation, what happened.

You are also welcome to emphasize again and again that there is no right or wrong here and that it is really only a matter of perception and observation.

To get started with meditation practice, the following meditations are great for children:

"I breathe ... in, I breathe ... out" meditation
This meditation is about the child becoming aware of what they want, how they want to feel, what they need right now, and at the same time letting go of what they no longer need, no longer want, what no longer serves them and wants to be processed or completed.

The meditation can be done in the morning, then the child can focus especially on what he wants for the day, what his needs are and what he needs to get through the day well, and what he does not want to take with him into the day, what he wants to let go and let go.

In the evening, meditation can be helpful to process what you have experienced, let go of all the experiences, let go of what is still bothering you, and take what it takes to end the day well.

Ask your child in advance of this meditation, get into conversation and let him tell you what moves him. If he or she wants to tell you, remember the individual points and then guide him or her through the meditation:

To do this, sit together on a meditation cushion or a conventional pillow or lie down. Depending on how it is most comfortable for your child and how the breath can flow well and freely.

Offer your child to close his eyes so that he can concentrate fully on himself and his inner self and avoid unnecessary distractions. Ultimately, however, it is the child who decides whether or not to close his or her eyes.

<u>Say the following meditation for your child. Feel free to read the text or use it freely:</u>

"Now direct your attention entirely to your breath ....

... notice how the air flows through your nose or mouth into your chest and abdomen when you inhale ...

... and leaves your body the same way when you exhale.

Take three more conscious breaths ...

The next time you inhale, imagine inhaling ....

*Put **one of** the positive words here that your child named ahead of time, or find one yourself if your child is too young to name it so precisely yourself. Examples: Calm/ Relaxation/ Joy/ Love/ Serenity/ Gratitude/ Trust/ Patience/ Peace.*

As you exhale ... breathe out and let it go.

*(Put **one** of the negative words here that your child named ahead of time, or find one yourself if your child is too young to name it so precisely yourself. Examples: Anger/rage/fighting/bullying/fear/worry/restlessness/unhappiness).*

> *Make sure that when you inhale and exhale, you use two terms that match each other as closely as possible, e.g. inhale: peace - exhale: anger/fight or inhale: joy - exhale: worry.*
>
> *Repeat this until all of your child's previously mentioned words have been used. If there were very few, you can use them several times in a row.*
>
> Now you have absorbed everything you wanted for yourself and for this day/evening, and you were able to let go of what you wanted to let go....
>
> ... now let three more breaths flow easily ...
>
> ... and then come back into the room ...
>
> ... open your eyes ...
>
> ... stretch yourself ...

Sun Rays Movement Meditation

In this meditation, the focus is on movement and imagination. Through the recurring sequence and with a little practice, your child no longer has to think much, can perceive the flow and thus internalize the taking in, accepting and letting go.

Starting position: Stand

1. Raise arms above head and stretch in position, speaking the text:

"We're reaching out to the sun."

2. Bring hands together above your head.

"We're catching the sun's rays."

3. Put your hands on your head.

"The sun's rays warm our heads."

4. Put your hands on your face.

"The sun's rays warm our faces."

5. Place hands on the heart.

"The sun's rays warm our hearts."

6. Put your hands on your stomach.

"The sun's rays warm our bellies."

7. Squat down and put your hands on the floor in front of you.

"We give the sun's rays to the earth."

This sequence can be repeated several times. Depending on how often the child wants to do it, it can be repeated from 1 to 5 times.

Mindfulness - a holistic gift

At this point, you surely realize that mindfulness can be a wonderful gift for your child, but also for you as a companion. A gift that can have a positive impact on your child's life, family life and the entire environment in a holistic way. Your child only needs to reach out, open the gift little by little and unwrap and enjoy the individual wonderful effects one by one.

I very much hope that you have realized one thing through the book, namely that for your child and yourself in this time characterized by fast pace, busyness and also pressure to succeed and perform, rest and deceleration are urgently needed for relaxation. Only in the small breaks and in the very conscious and mindful moments body and mind come to rest. In these moments the soul can dangle.

Nothing is better suited to perceiving and observing these moments than mindfulness exercises that bring your child into the here and now and allow him or her to arrive fully in the moment.

I wish you and your child lots of fun trying out, experimenting, experiencing and perceiving.

www.ingramcontent.com/pod-product-compliance
Lightning Source LLC
Chambersburg PA
CBHW031411160726
47993CB00003B/1192